Your Brain:
UNDERSTANDING YOUR BODY'S
CONTROL CENTER

BY JEFF SZPIRGLAS AND
DANIELLE SAINT-ONGE

CRABTREE
PUBLISHING COMPANY
WWW.CRABTREEBOOKS.COM

CRABTREE
PUBLISHING COMPANY
WWW.CRABTREEBOOKS.COM

Authors: Jeff Szpirglas, Danielle Saint-Onge

Series Research and Development: Reagan Miller

Editors: Janine Deschenes, Kenneth Lane

Proofreader: Wendy Scavuzzo

Design: Margaret Amy Salter

Photo research: Margaret Amy Salter

Production coordinator and

  Prepress technician: Margaret Amy Salter, Abigail Smith

Print coordinator: Katherine Berti

Consultant: Kenneth Lane, Bioscientist and Science Writer and Editor

Photo Credits
br=bottom right

Shutterstock: ©Yuri Turkov p 39 (br)

All other images from Shutterstock

Library and Archives Canada Cataloguing in Publication

Szpirglas, Jeff, author
     Your brain : understanding your body's control center /
Jeff Szpirglas, Danielle Saint-Onge.

(Exploring the brain)
Includes bibliographical references and index.
Issued in print and electronic formats.
ISBN 978-0-7787-3509-0 (hardcover).--
ISBN 978-0-7787-3513-7 (softcover).--
ISBN 978-1-4271-1997-1 (HTML)

     1. Brain--Juvenile literature. 2. Brain--Physiology--Juvenile
literature. I. Saint-Onge, Danielle, author II. Title.

QP376.S97 2017   j612.8'2   C2017-906545-9
                                          C2017-906546-7

Library of Congress Cataloging-in-Publication Data

Names: Szpirglas, Jeff, author. | Saint-Onge, Danielle, 1982- author.
Title: Your brain : understanding your body's control center /
     Jeff Szpirglas and Danielle Saint-Onge.
Description: New York, New York : Crabtree Publishing Company,
     [2018] | Series: Exploring the brain |
     Includes bibliographical references and index.
Identifiers: LCCN 2017059664 (print) | LCCN 2017060177 (ebook) |
     ISBN 9781427119971 (Electronic HTML) |
     ISBN 9780778735090 (reinforced library binding) |
     ISBN 9780778735137 (pbk.)
Subjects: LCSH: Brain--Localization of functions--Juvenile literature. |
     Brain--Anatomy--Juvenile literature. | Senses and sensation--Juvenile
     literature.
Classification: LCC QP385 (ebook) | LCC QP385 .S97 2018 (print) |
     DDC 612.8/2--dc23
LC record available at https://lccn.loc.gov/2017059664

Crabtree Publishing Company

www.crabtreebooks.com   1-800-387-7650

Printed in the U.S.A./022018/CG20171220

Published in Canada
Crabtree Publishing
616 Welland Ave.
St. Catharines, Ontario
L2M 5V6

Published in the United States
Crabtree Publishing
PMB 59051
350 Fifth Avenue, 59th Floor
New York, New York 10118

Published in the United Kingdom
Crabtree Publishing
Maritime House
Basin Road North, Hove
BN41 1WR

Published in Australia
Crabtree Publishing
3 Charles Street
Coburg North
VIC, 3058

Table of Contents

CHAPTER 1

BRAIN BASICS

Open up the back of any computer, and you'll find the CPU, or Central Processing Unit. This tiny piece of hardware processes, or makes sense of, all of the instructions in the programs and files you use in your computer. It's what makes your computer do the work you need it to do!

The computer is modeled after nature's greatest CPU—your brain. Stored safely behind your skull and a layer of protective fluid is your brain, weighing in at 3.3 pounds (1.5 kilograms). Some scientists estimate that every second, your body is sending 1.5 million bits of information to your brain for processing.

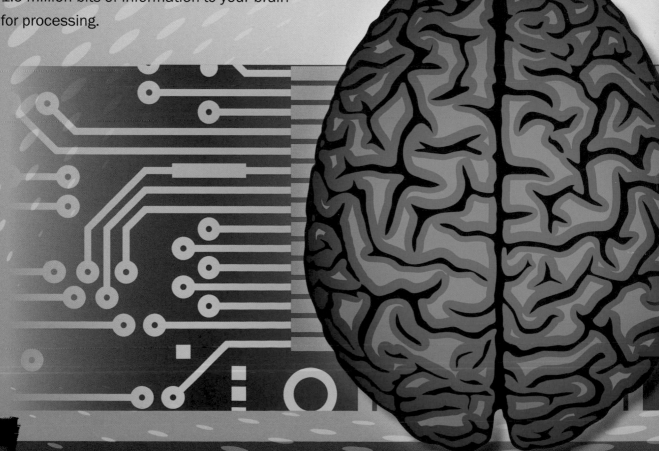

Your brain processes the information it receives when your body reacts to **stimuli**. These are the things in our environment that our senses react to. Stimuli are interpreted by **sensory receptors** on our skin, eyes, tongue, ears, and nose, which send messages to and from the brain. Your brain receives information from these receptors, processes it, and will either store that information as a memory, or send a message back to parts of your body to respond immediately—which explains why you wouldn't leave your hands on a hot stove for long—it hurts!

Even now, as you read this page, the sensory receptors on your skin are telling you how much pressure is needed to hold the book in your hand without crumpling the paper. They're telling you how quickly your eyes need to track across this line of text so that your brain can recognize letters, words, and sentences—and turn them into something that makes sense to you.

So how do your sensory receptors help you react to stimuli in your environment? First, let's get behind your skull to explore the inner workings of your brain.

Take a Deep Breath. Feels Good, Right?

Just like the control center of a computer uses a lot of energy, so does your brain. Your brain needs a lot of fuel to run, which is why it uses around one-quarter (25%) of the oxygen that you're breathing right now. What's the brain actually made of?

Fat Is Fab!

Most of the solid **matter** in your brain is made of fats. In fact, the good fat in your brain helps to build the **cell membranes** in your whole body, which is why a diet that includes good fats, such as the fats you get from fish and avocados, is important.

Brain Makeup

Your brain has around 100 billion neurons, or nerve cells. Can't picture how many that is? If you could tie them together, they'd form a rope that would reach all the way to the moon and back again. Not that you should try doing such a thing.

neuron

Neurons send messages to and from your brain and other parts of your body. They can be categorized in two ways. The **gray matter** of the brain consists of the cell bodies of neurons. The **white matter** is made up of the dendrites and axons of neurons that extend to neighboring neurons and carry signals between them (you can read more about neurons, dendrites, and axons on page 14).

Although it contains about 100 billion neurons, your brain is mostly composed of **glial cells**. There are around 1 trillion of them! These cells help make the messages that come from your neurons stronger. They also provide the **nutrients** that your neurons need to work.

glial cell

BRAIN BREAKDOWN
What's in a Brain?

Water 77–78%
Carbohydrates (Sugars) 1 %
Soluble Organic Substances 2%
Inorganic Salts 1%
Protein 8%
Lipids (Fats) 10–12%

CHAPTER 2

WITHIN the SKULL

Your brain isn't just a jelly-like mass that rests inside your head. There are a host of structures that make up the brain. Each one has specific abilities to complete different tasks.

Cerebrum

The cerebrum, or cerebral cortex, takes in messages from the body's sense organs and sensory structures. It's a massive feature of the brain, and there is more about it on pages 10–11.

Limbic System

This is the part of your brain responsible for controlling your emotional response. For example, if you react to a loud sound by jumping, this is your limbic system jumping into action. Your limbic system is made of two main structures that work together—the hippocampus and the amygdala.

Hypothalamus

The hypothalamus controls how your body releases **hormones** that help you grow, digest food, and do other things.

Hippocampus

The hippocampus is responsible for organizing and storing memories. It also helps you connect emotions to memories.

Pituitary Gland

A gland is an organ or group of cells that make substances that the body needs to function. The pituitary gland, which is about the size of a pea, makes growth hormone, which is responsible for the body's physical development, as well as making other hormones that control how other glands in the body work.

Thalamus

This part of the brain gets referred to as the brain's "relay station." It takes in tons of sensory information and sends it on to the cerebrum.

Amygdala

Your amygdala is the part of your brain that controls emotional reactions to stimuli and events.

DISPROVEN THEORIES

PHRENOLOGY

In the 1800s, there was a popular theory that stated that the shape of your skull and brain could determine your personality—such as how intelligent (or not) you were. Known as phrenology, this idea was started by a German doctor named Franz Joseph Gall (1758–1828). As a student, Gall observed that his intelligent peers had protruding eyes, and wondered if that part of the brain was larger. Today, we know there is no link between head shape or size and intelligence.

Cerebellum

This part of the brain, located near the back and bottom of the brain, coordinates the body's voluntary muscle functions to allow for good posture, balance, speech, and coordinated movement. It helps you to walk, jump, and move in a smooth and efficient way. It takes up around 10 percent of your brain's volume.

Reptilian Brain

This portion of your brain is made up of three structures: the **brainstem**, **pons**, and **medulla**. It controls your heart rate, breathing, and digestion. These are body functions that occur continuously and automatically, which means that they occur without our thinking about them.

The Cerebrum

About three-quarters of your brain's volume is taken up by your cerebrum, the largest structure in your brain. This structure includes the outer layer of the brain, called the cerebral cortex, which covers some of the inner parts of the brain you just learned about. It also includes some inner parts of the brain such as the hippocampus. Looking at the cerebral cortex on these pages, you'll notice ridges, called **gyri**, and folds between these ridges, called **sulci**. These folds are important, because they allow a large amount of matter to fit into the space of your skull. How large is this amount of brain tissue? If you were to pop that brain tissue out of your head and spread it out, your cerebral cortex would cover an area slightly larger than the two pages of this book that you're now looking at.

Prefrontal Cortex

This part of the brain allows you to make decisions, think critically, and learn complex new things.

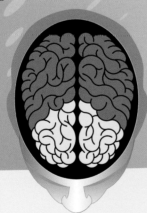

MOTOR

SENSORY

Frontal Lobes

Located above and behind your eyes, this section of your brain is involved in the coordination of your movements.

Motor Cortex

This part of the brain sends signals to your muscles to contract or relax. Planning on putting this book down to get up and take a break? Prepare to receive a signal from your primary motor cortex.

Sensory Cortex

There are actually two sensory cortices. The primary sensory cortex receives messages relating to the sense of touch. The messages are then processed in the association cortex as part of the recognition of objects and events. This acts as a type of "library" of objects and events that has been built from previous sensory encounters with them, such as recognizing a cactus from its spines or a comb from its teeth.

Parietal Lobes

This part of your brain controls your movement and your spatial awareness, or how you are aware of your own body in relation to the space and objects around it.

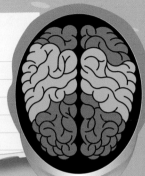

Occipital Lobes

These take in information from your eyes and process it.

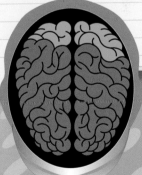

Temporal Lobes

These areas take in sounds and process language. It's this part of the brain that contains the hippocampus, which stores and preserves long-term memories, such as information learned at school, or locations of objects and people.

II

Two Halves

Seen from above, your brain can be divided into two halves, called hemispheres. These two hemispheres control different body functions. There's a fascinating "flip" of control going on here. Your brain's right hemisphere controls movement for the left side of your body, while your brain's left hemisphere controls movement for the right side. Try raising your left hand, and know that it's your brain's right side that's in charge.

What are some other differences between the left and right hemispheres?

LEFT HEMISPHERE

- The left hemisphere processes details of objects that you see.

- In most adults (70–95%), the left hemisphere is the language center of the brain.

RIGHT HEMISPHERE

- The right hemisphere is believed to control nonverbal spatial skills such as body movement.

- This hemisphere processes the shape of objects.

- Your ability to detect tone of voice or body language (happy, angry) is in the right hemisphere.

Corpus Callosum

This structure is a bundle of around 200 to 250 nerve fibers that join the two hemispheres of the brain. It might be compared to headphones that play on both sides of your brain. Failure of the corpus callosum to develop completely is called agenesis of the callosum. It can delay motor control of the body, making walking difficult. It can also delay speech and make it difficult to communicate with other people.

CREATIVE VS LOGICAL HEMISPHERES

Try searching the Internet, and you'll probably come across many articles that state that the two hemispheres of the brain are separately responsible for logical and creative thinking. You would be likely to read that "left brain thinkers" are analytical, while "right brain thinkers" are more creative. That sounds fascinating, but there isn't any real science to back it up. In fact, studies show that both hemispheres of the brain are used for many tasks that involve both logic and creativity.

BRAIN LAB

On their own, the words below may not mean much. But try saying them over and over again. Can you find the real phrase?

THIS GUY'S THEY'LL HYMN IT

A: The sky's the limit.

Wernicke's Area and Broca's Area

These two areas of the left hemisphere are important for how we process, or understand, language. They are named after a pair of neurologists, Paul Broca and Karl Wernicke, who discovered that damage to portions of the left hemisphere caused speech and language problems.

CHAPTER 3

Getting on Your NERVES

It's impossible to talk about how your control center works without exploring neurons—the nerve cells that send signals, or messages, to and from the brain and other parts of the body. You've got around 100 billion of them inside of you right now. But how do they communicate?

Neurons can be broken down into three main parts. The **cell body** is in charge of the neuron's activity. Projecting from the cell body are extensions known as **dendrites**, that resemble tree roots. These receive signals from other neurons and pass those messages to the cell body. Also projecting from the cell body of the neuron is the **axon**, a single, long fiber that sends signals to other neurons. Covering the axon is a fatty substance called **myelin**. This protects the axon and may help in speeding up the signals sent through the axon to other neurons.

A **synapse** is the small gap between the end of an axon of one neuron and the beginning of the dendrites of the next neuron. The synapse contains **neurotransmitters**. These substances act as messengers between the end of the axon of one neuron and the beginning of the dendrite of a neighboring neuron, as these neurons transmit messages from the brain to the body and vice versa.

synapse

How fast are the signals sent through the axon? It is estimated that the speed of such a signal can be as slow as 1 mile (1.6 kph) per hour.

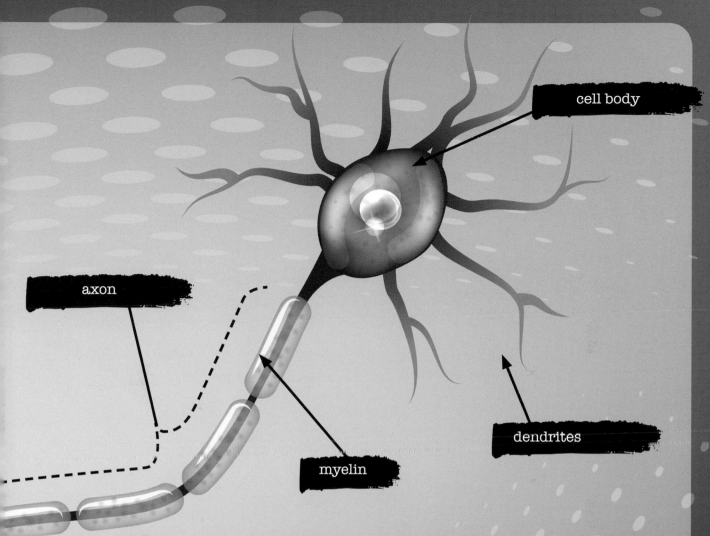

cell body

axon

myelin

dendrites

Most of the cells in your body are constantly dying and being replaced, such as your skin cells, which are continually being shed, even as you sit and read this book. But many neurons aren't replaced when they die. When brain neurons die and are not replaced, the process is called pruning, as when someone prunes dead or unruly branches of a tree. If they are not being used, your body lets neurons die out.

...and as fast as 335 miles (540 kph) per hour in the case of some myelinated neurons.

Neurons are also among the longest cells in your body. While some neurons are less than half an inch (1 cm) long, other neurons have axons that may be more than a foot (30 cm) long. There is an axon from the spine to the foot that extends to more than 3 feet (1 m) long.

Nerve are Connectors

Your nerves are what connect your brain to all of the other systems in your body—such as your circulatory system, which controls your blood flow to the organs that need it; skeletal system, which supports your body; digestive system, which turns food into the energy you need to live; and respiratory system, which brings oxygen into the body through the lungs.
In other words, no nerves, no control!

GET NEURONIC

Not all neurons are created equal. They are specially designed for different tasks.

Motor Neurons
These carry signals away from your central nervous system to regulate your muscles and glands. This helps your body to function properly and to respond appropriately to its environment.

motor neuron

Sensory Neurons
These neurons send signals toward your central nervous system from your eyes, ears, and other sensory organs, and from sensory receptors in your skin for touch, heat, and cold.

sensory neuron

Interneurons
Mainly found in the spinal cord and brain, interneurons send signals back and forth between sensory and motor neurons. These complete the circuit that allows the Central Nervous System (see page 19) to communicate with the sensory and motor neurons.

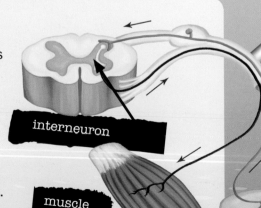

interneuron

muscle

skin

Most of your nerve cells are found deep within your body—but not all! Right near the surface of your skin, near the elbow, is your **ulnar nerve**. This sends signals about the sensations in your fourth and fifth fingers, and controls some of your hand movements. But if you bump your ulnar nerve against your humerus (the bone that runs from your elbow to the shoulder), you'll notice a weird tingling sensation running down your arm. This is what's known as bumping your "funny bone." The funny thing is, there is no funny bone. It's just the sensation of the ulnar nerve getting bumped.

funny bone

How do neurons make muscles work? It's a two-way street. Your brain sends signals through your brain stem and down your spinal cord. These signals then pass from the spinal cord into specific muscles, controlling their actions. Once the muscles contract, as in making a fist, receptors in the muscles send signals to the brain, telling it what the muscles are doing. The brain then uses these signals to appropriately increase or decrease the force with which the muscles are acting, as in making a tight or loose fist.

BRAIN LAB

SYNAPSE TAG

Want to model how a synapse works, and do it by playing a game of Octopus?

The goal of the game is to have players act as neurotransmitters. They'll need to move across a synapse, from the end of an axon to a dendrite, without getting caught by an **enzyme** that exists in the synapse and destroys neurotransmitters. A few other players, in the space that represents the synapse between the axon and the dendrite, will play the role of the enzyme.

Start by marking spaces on either side of the playing area as the axon and the dendrite. Have most players start as the neurotransmitters. They must start in a zone set up to be an axon. A few other players will be enzymes, and start in the space between the zones. This space is the synapse.

Neurotransmitter players run across the synapse trying not to get tagged by the enzyme. If tagged, players must return to the axon and can only play again on the next round. A player who represents a neurotransmitter and safely reaches the dendrite without getting tagged represents the safe arrival of a nerve signal at the dendrite.

Your Nervous System

Together, all the nerve cells in your body make up your nervous system. This system is what we use to interact with the world around us as our brains constantly communicate with our sensory organs, such as our skin, ears, and tongues. Information is taken in through the senses and triggers a reaction. The reaction could be something as simple as enjoying the feel of your hands touching a cat's soft fur, the gag reflex that happens when you smell spoiled food, or the feeling of needing to go to the bathroom!

Central Nervous System

Your brain is a part of the central nervous system (CNS), which also includes your spinal cord. This is a thick strand of nerve tissue containing more than 13 million neurons that connects your brain to the rest of your body. It's around 18 inches (46 cm) long. That's just about the width of this book if you opened it up and laid it flat. Because it's made up of such sensitive material, your CNS is shielded by bones, such as your skull, and your backbone, which protects the spinal cord.

18 inches (46 cm)

Peripheral Nervous System

While the CNS has fairly straightforward parts, the peripheral nervous system (PNS) looks a lot more complicated, like a road map gone wild. The PNS is made up of neurons that join parts of your body to the spinal cord through nerve fibers. These nerve fibers are what allow your fingers to feel the pages of this book, or to sense the temperature around you...unless you're reading this in a snowstorm!

The neurons running through your PNS have different roles. Afferent neurons carry information from your sensory organs, skin, and other parts of your body to your brain. Efferent neurons carry impulses from your CNS to your limbs and organs, such as the impulses that control heartbeat, breathing, and motions of the arms and legs.

PUT YOUR BRAIN TO IT!

How do our bodies depend on neurons? Give evidence from the book to support your answer.

Voluntary or Involuntary

Different parts of your nervous system control your voluntary and involuntary actions. Voluntary means done by choice. Your voluntary nervous system, or **somatic nervous system**, is a part of the PNS that takes signals from the CNS to your muscles. The signals that come from your CNS are often determined by your senses. For example, when your alarm clock blares to life in the morning, your sense of hearing hears the alarm and you make a decision to get out of bed. Your brain sends a signal to your muscles to roll out of bed and get ready for school. All of these actions are determined by the voluntary nervous system.

Involuntary means done without realizing it, or without consciously choosing to do it. The involuntary nervous system, or **autonomic nervous system**, is the means by which your brain controls functions of your body that occur automatically, such as your heartbeat or the contractions of the muscles that control your breathing. The autonomic nervous system does this by passing signals from your brain to these parts of your body.

If you're the sort of person who slams a tired hand down on the snooze button, that's yet another example of your voluntary nervous system in action.

The autonomic nervous system can be broken down into three parts:

Sympathetic Nervous System

This system is responsible for what is known as the "fight or flight response." It increases your breathing rate, constricts blood vessels, and reduces the size of your pupils, as well as exerts other effects when your body experiences stress. It does this when you're awake and active and when you dream during sleep.

Parasympathetic Nervous System

This system has almost the opposite effect of the sympathetic nervous system. It slows your heart rate, decreases the size of your pupils, and relaxes some of your muscles.

Enteric Nervous System (ENS)

Your digestive system has its own specialized nervous system, called the enteric nervous system. It helps control how you digest your food—from your stomach to your intestines.

CHAPTER 4

Getting to Know the SENSES

So Sensitive

Touch, smell, taste, hearing, and sight—the five senses that you use every day—are the result of a special group of neurons called sensory receptors. Changes in the environment, called stimuli, cause these receptors to react. The stimuli that cause this may be a sudden, loud volume coming through your headphones, the odor of milk gone bad, or a finger being jabbed by a thorn.

SENSORY CONNECTIONS

By about the age of three months, you're clearly able to tell the difference between sound, taste, touch, smell, and sight. But for around 1 in every 20,000 people (some estimates suggest even 1 in 200), some parts of the sensory cortex may get cross-wired. Are you the kind of person who sees numbers as colors? You might have **synesthesia**, which means that you have multiple connections around the brain areas that have to do with the senses. Synesthetes might hear colors, taste shapes, or feel sounds. Famous synesthetes include composer Franz Liszt and singer-songwriter Mary J. Blige.

There are three main types of sensory receptors at work in your body.

Exteroceptors respond to things that happen outside your body. They are responsible for your feelings of touch, such as pressure against your skin or feelings of pain, along with your hearing, smell, taste, and sight.

Interoceptors are sensory receptors inside your body. They respond to stimuli such as feeling hunger or thirst.

Finally, there are proprioceptors, also located inside the body in your skeletal muscles and joints. These are responsible for keeping you balanced while moving.

Exteroceptors, interoceptors, and proprioceptors work together in harmony to interpret information and send it to your brain. Walking down a hallway means you need to use the exteroceptors for sight, to make sure that you don't bump into anything on your way. You also use the exteroceptors for touch—how fast are you walking? How hard are your feet hitting the floor? As you walk, you're also using the proprioceptors in your feet and legs, to keep you balanced so that you don't fall.

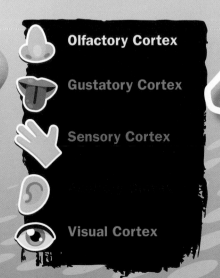

Olfactory Cortex

Gustatory Cortex

Sensory Cortex

Visual Cortex

For every sensory area, there is a corresponding cortex in the cerebrum.

Setting Sights on You

Right now, you're tracking the words along this page with your eyes. You'd think your eyes are moving in a straight line, but instead, they're making short, jerky movements as you scan the letters and the words. Your eyes might take in the image of this paragraph, but it's in your brain where the words are processed and you understand what the words mean. That's because your eyes and brain work together, like a sensory tag team.

How it Works

Light rays reflect from objects around you, and enter the eye through the **cornea**. The light is bent as it passes through the pupil, and is further shaped as it passes through your eye's lens. The lens focuses the light on the **retina** at the back of your eye. It's there that millions of nerve cells, known as **photoreceptors**—also called rods and cones because of their shape—help you notice color and motion.

cornea

pupil

retina

photoreceptors, or rods and cones

Braille Brain Buster

Studies of vision have been done with blind people who read with Braille, which is a system of raised dots on paper that represent the letters of the alphabet. It spells out words, sentences, and paragraphs, like those you are reading now. When people read with Braille, they use their fingertips to identify the letters and words they're reading by touching the raised dots. When people read Braille, they activate the parts of the brain that respond to touch. But some researchers have found that touching the dots of the Braille system activates the visual cortex, which is the part of the brain that recognizes visual stimuli in people with normal eyesight. It's still unclear if this has to do with Braille's organization, or if in blind people the brain area normally used for sight is reprocessed for reading Braille.

From there, the light is converted into signals that are sent to the brain along an **optic nerve**. In the brain, the images in the retina are processed by the visual cortex, allowing you to see. Your brain makes sense of the images to help you recognize what you're seeing.

BRAIN LAB

EYE SPY

Your brain does a great job filling in blank spaces. Want to prove it? Try reading these numbers from right to left with your left eye, starting from 1. Everything seems okay, right? Try it again. But this time, put a hand over your right eye. Does the face disappear as you count, then reappear again?

9 8 7 6 5 4 3 2 1

You've Got the Touch!

You can't turn off your sense of touch. Your sense of touch is part of your somatosensory system, or body-sensing system. It is concerned with the sense of touch and perception of pain, temperature, pressure, movement, and vibration. It helps you to stand and walk, feel your way around, and know that you've touched a hot pot handle!

How it Works

Built into your skin are **mechanoreceptors**. These are your body's special sensory receptors for touch. These receptors are most sensitive on places such as your lips, feet, and fingertips. At the age of 10, you've got around 50 touch receptors for every square millimeter of your skin. Every fingertip has more than 3,000 touch receptors alone! These neurons can stretch under the pressure of just a drop of rain. As they are activated, the neurons fire, sending their messages to various nerve fibers. The signals travel through the fibers, along the spine and brain stem, and through the thalamus, right to your **somatosensory cortex** in the brain.

Your sense of touch works at the same time as your other senses. For example, when you picked up this book, your senses of sight and touch worked together. Your brain told you when to stop moving your hand toward the book, and how to curl your fingers around the book to pick it up.

PUT YOUR BRAIN TO IT!

Why is feeling pain important? Can you share a time in your life when feeling pain was helpful?

No Pain, No Gain!

You might not like feeling pain, but it can literally save your skin (especially if you've ever touched the red hot coil of a stove). How does it work? In your skin, muscles, bones, and joints, you have special sensory cells called **nociceptors**. You've got several different kinds of nociceptors that respond to different signals, such as stretching, pinching, or cutting. When nociceptors are activated, they send messages that activate nerves in the skin. These nerves are designed to send signals of pain to your brain. Once the signals sent by nociceptors are picked up by the thalamus and relayed to the cerebral cortex, your brain sends the response:

Take your hand off that hot coil!

Feeling the Heat

Those nociceptors responsible for sending pain signals are also helpful when dealing with temperatures. Your skin also has **thermoreceptors**, which are nerve cells sensitive to temperature. These receptors have **proteins** that can change their activity according to the temperature to which they are exposed.

early stage of frostbite

There are "cold receptors" and "warm receptors." After being exposed to temperatures above 113°F (45°C), or 32°F (0°C) below freezing, these nociceptors will signal your brain, telling you to seek warmth (or cold...).

Good Vibrations

From the tiniest drop of a pin to the most blaring power chords from the heavy-metal music on the radio, we are immersed in a world of sounds. As they do with touch and sight, our brains interpret sounds from the physical world to help us do everything from crossing the street safely to carrying out important conversations.

How it Works

As objects around us vibrate, they create sound waves. These waves are picked up by our ears. Sounds are first collected by the dish of your outer ear, which helps to concentrate, or focus, the vibrations. Next, sounds are carried down your ear canal to the eardrum, a thin layer of tissue that is made to vibrate by the sounds sent down your ear canal.

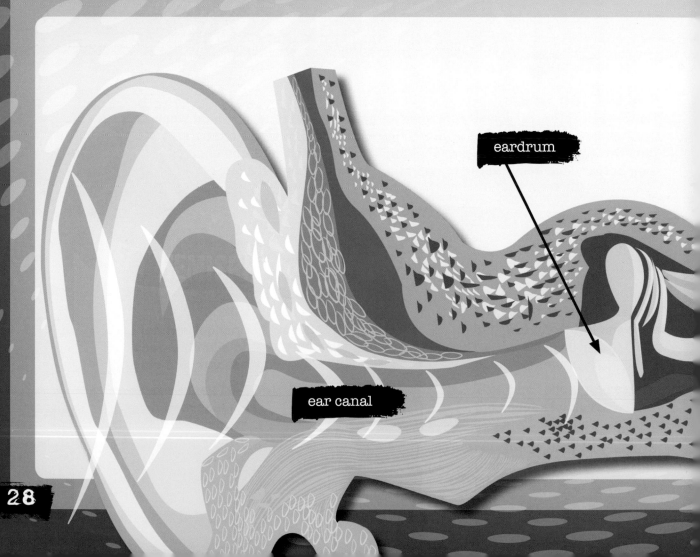

eardrum

ear canal

It is interesting that each hemisphere of your brain treats the sounds of spoken language differently. The left side of your brain can pick out parts of speech as phonemes, the individual parts of sounds that make up words (for example, the word "cat" can be broken up into the sounds c-a-t).

The right side picks up on the melodic portion of talk, such as pitch, volume, and rhythm. Studies have indicated that Wernickle's area is the part of your brain that decodes speech. And speaking and writing are processed in Broca's area.

On the other side of your eardrum is your middle ear. There, tiny bones begin to vibrate as the energy of the vibrations of your eardrum is transferred into the fluid of an organ called the **cochlea**. Within the cochlea, nerve cells interpret the sound as signals.

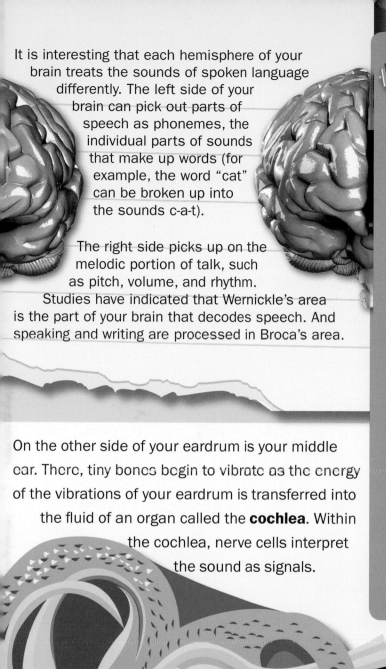

cochlea

BRAIN LAB

TRY THIS BRAIN WORKOUT!

Educators Paul E. Dennison and Gail Dennison developed a unique set of exercises that help to activate both hemispheres of your brain at the same time. The goal is to increase communication and information flow between the hemispheres. By doing these exercises, you can improve your reading and writing skills. There are 26 basic exercises in total.
Here are two you can try:

Calf Pump:
Extend your right leg behind you and as the heel is touching the floor, hold it down for approximately 8 seconds and release. Repeat 7 or 8 times, then repeat with the other leg.

Cross Crawl
Stand or sit. Put the right hand across the body to the left knee as you raise it, then do the same thing for the left hand on the right knee. You must do this either sitting or standing for about 2 minutes.

These signals are then sent down the **auditory nerve** to the brain's auditory cortex. There, your brain tells you what you are hearing.

Take a Whiff

Smell and taste are known as the chemical senses. This means that instead of a sense that responds to something physical in the environment, such as a sound, these senses react to chemicals around us, whether they're dissolved in a liquid (taste) or in the air (smell, also known as olfaction).

How it Works

Take a deep breath in through your nose. In addition to sending oxygen into your lungs, you probably got a sense of the smell of the room you're sitting in. At the back of your nasal cavity are millions of sensory receptors, called **olfactory neurons.**

olfactory bulb

olfactory neurons

These neurons have hair-like extensions called cilia that are covered in a layer of slimy **mucus**. As you breathe, chemicals in the air dissolve in the mucus, and reach the cilia—whether the chemicals that do this are those that produce the smell of fresh food cooking in the cafeteria, or the awful stench of a garbage can on a hot summer day.

The olfactory neurons in your nose send signals to your **olfactory bulb**, located above your nasal cavity. From there, these signals go to your olfactory cortex, where you can identify the odor.

For many years, it had been estimated that your brain has a strong memory for different smells—up to 10,000 of them. But at least one recent study suggests that humans are able to identify more than 1 trillion smells.

Taster's Choice

You might love the taste of a freshly barbecued burger (unless meat isn't your thing, in which case, we'd be happy to offer you a Portobello mushroom burger in its place). The idea of chomping down on one might even make your mouth water as you read this, which is good— saliva is needed to help taste your food. But so is your nose. When you recognize a food's flavor, your senses of smell and taste are working together.

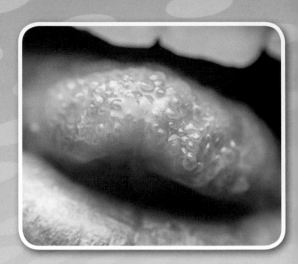

How It Works

Zoom in on your tongue and you'll find around 10,000 bumpy taste buds. Each bud has around 50 to 100 **taste receptor cells**. Each cell contains a tiny hair that pushes through a pore to the tongue's surface, which is coated in saliva.

As you sip a drink or chew your food, the chemicals responsible for its flavor are mixed with the saliva that coats your tongue, and make contact with the taste buds, where they can touch these tiny hairs.

When they come into contact with the taste receptor cells in your taste buds, the chemicals in the food cause these cells to release neurotransmitter substances and to send taste messages to your brain.

thalamus

medulla

gustatory cortex

These messages follow three pathways, along the **facial nerve**, the **glossopharyngeal nerve**, and the **vagus nerve**—arriving at the medulla, then the thalamus and **gustatory cortex** of your brain. Other taste-nerve fibers are connected in your brain to the hypothalamus and your limbic system. This is where your brain determines whether a flavor is yummy or gross. These connections are what make you say, "Wow, I love pickled tongue sandwiches," or "Yuck! Pickled tongue sandwiches? I'd rather hurl!"

Age and Taste

As you age, the number of taste receptors in your tongue decreases, meaning that you're less likely to taste things as intensely. Children and adults also tend to have different sensory appreciations for flavors. Young children seem to have a higher threshold for enjoying sugar and sweets, but are more sensitive to bitter tastes. In fact, some research has suggested that sugar can even be used as a natural painkiller for younger children.

DISPROVEN THEORIES

TONGUE MAP

Humans are able to break tastes down into five categories: sour, salty, bitter, sweet, and umami (oo-MAH-mee), which is a savory flavor found in mushrooms and parmesan cheese. For years, a myth circulated that different regions of the tongue were responsible for picking up the various tastes. For example, the tip of the tongue is sensitive to sweet tastes and the back is sensitive to bitter. But tongue maps such as the one below are not proven by science.

Tasty Choices
With five different taste categories, humans can recognize around 100,000 different flavors. But can you get them all as ice cream flavors?

CHAPTER 5

RESPONDING and REMEMBERING

Boo!

Did seeing that image on this page startle you? A startle is your body's fast response to a sudden, intense stimulus (a sudden movement, such as something flying at you, a sudden loud sound, such as a clap of thunder, or a jump scare in a good horror film). In short, it's your body's way of protecting itself against injury by gearing up to protect against a sudden attack, and readying yourself for "fight or flight" mode. And all of this happens before you can even have time to figure out what's going on.

How does your startle reflex work? In an auditory startle, signals from your ear canal set events in motion. Your thalamus, which takes in sensory information, gets the message of a sudden fright from your senses. It sends a signal to your amygdala to start your startle response. Connections also fire between the amygdala and the **locus coeruleus**—a part of your brain that gets you ready for that fight-or-flight response. So, when hearing a sudden noise, your muscles will tense, and you'll hunch your body, contracting your head, neck, arms, and legs—all within a traction of a second.

Pupils dialate, or get bigger

Senses may become sharper

Heart rate increases

Breathing rate increases

Body begins to sweat

Non-essential body functions, such as the digestive system, relax or slow down to allow more energy for emergency body functions

Muscles tense and body contracts into a hunch shape

Can't Stop Startling

A famous story tells how Charles Darwin tried to hold back his own startle reaction in a visit to the zoo. He went over to a container that held a type of snake called a puff adder. Knowing that a wall of glass would keep him safe if the snake struck, he tried to suppress, or stop, his startle reflex. Could the world-famous explorer and thinker hold back his startle reflex? Fat chance. "My will and reason were powerless," he went on to say. Even knowing you're going to get startled won't help your brain from triggering a response to a sudden sound or action.

puff adder snake

This is Your Brain on Fear

Your brain controls your senses, but also your reactions to the messages being sent from your sense organs and receptors. Memories may help drive an emotional response to a sensory message, which is sent from your brain to other parts of your body—whether you're flushing with embarrassment or crying with sadness. Take, for example, the emotion of fear. Your brain uses stored memories extensively when a fearful response is triggered. Here's how it works.

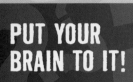

PUT YOUR BRAIN TO IT!

What are some of the effects that a fight-or-flight response has on the body? Pick one effect. How do you think this would help you avoid danger?

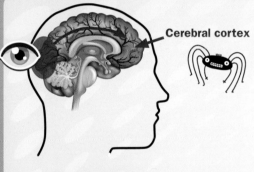

Cerebral cortex

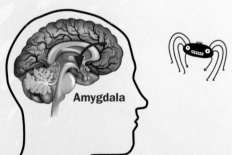

Amygdala

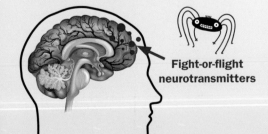

Fight-or-flight neurotransmitters

Anatomy of a Scare

Fear really begins in the cortices of your brain, such as your visual cortex, located at the back of the brain, which helps you process what you see.

Let's say you see a spider crawling on the wall. Afraid of spiders? Your visual cortex sends a message of fear to your cerebral cortex. Then the message is taken to your amygdala and the insular cortex or insula of the brain, which help process your emotion of fear.

The amygdala helps to determine whether an object or event can do you harm. This sometimes allows you to regulate, or control, your emotional and physical response to danger.

If spiders really freak you out, now your cerebral cortex goes to work. It produces a group of neurotransmitters that get your body primed for fight-or-flight mode.

But wait! What if that spider is just a speck of dirt? Your brain produces a type of acid, which reduces the excitability of neurons throughout the nervous system, helping you to calm down and get back to your regular body functions.

FIGHT OR FLIGHT

One of the ingredients in your fight-or-flight reaction is adrenaline—a hormone produced by the adrenal glands atop your kidneys. When pumped through the body, adrenaline gears the body to be primed for something physical—whether to face a threat or run away.

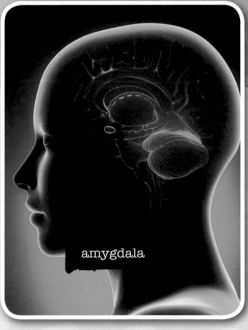

Scared Silly?

Some of us love getting scared, whether by riding roller coasters, watching horror movies, or doing something else that causes us fear. When we feel scared, our pituitary gland releases **endorphins**, which are chemicals that ease pain and induce feelings of pleasure.

THE AMYGDALA

YOUR FEAR-O-METER

One of the functions of the amygdala, located near the front of the temporal lobe of the brain, is to connect emotions with memories stored in the brain. Say you've been afraid of spiders since one walked across your leg. When you see a spider again, the amygdala connects back to that stored, long-term memory (more on that later). It then sends a signal to your body to be ready to react to the spider as a potential danger. It does this in a few thousandths of a second.

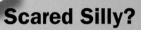

amygdala

You Must Remember This

Your memory drives your emotions, such as fear, and also your ability to complete daily tasks such as tying your shoes. For instance, you'd hardly be afraid of the idea of ghosts or spooky haunted houses if you hadn't had a fearful experience of being freaked out on Halloween or seen some scary movie. But how does your brain create and store the memories that drive your emotions, or that help you get through the daily grind?

$$2a-(4)=$$
$$25-(2y)=$$
$$3 \times 8=$$

Short or Long?

When we talk about memory, we can divide our memories into categories. Short-term memory can store several things at a time, but only for a short period. When learning something new in school for the first time, your brain tends to make use of your short-term memory, because it can store many things at once. For many people, your short-term memory can store around seven things at a time. But this number can vary from one person to another, depending on the type of information being stored, and on the learning situation. Still, that's why teachers tend to "chunk" information in lessons into small, digestible bits, and have you repeat and retry new activities over a period of time. This helps turn the short-term memories into longer-lasting ones.

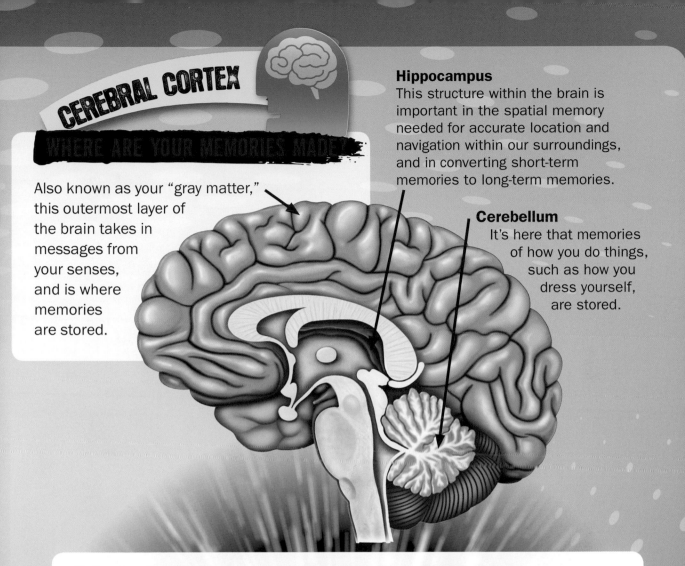

CEREBRAL CORTEX

Also known as your "gray matter," this outermost layer of the brain takes in messages from your senses, and is where memories are stored.

Hippocampus
This structure within the brain is important in the spatial memory needed for accurate location and navigation within our surroundings, and in converting short-term memories to long-term memories.

Cerebellum
It's here that memories of how you do things, such as how you dress yourself, are stored.

A Long Time Ago, In a Galaxy Far, Far Away...

It's one of the most famous movie lines ever, and at slightly more than seven words, a good example of how short-term memory works. The first time you heard those words, your brain would have been firing signals from clusters of neurons that recognized each word you heard or read. When one of these clusters of neurons fires, it prevents other clusters from firing, which would scramble the message carried by a series of words. Once all of the neurons have fired, your brain will create a pathway to remember the sequence of words in a message.

But the longer a phrase or expression gets, the harder it is for the neuron clusters to keep the other neurons from firing. Weaker pathways are formed, and you can't create a long-term memory of the sequence of words in a message without it being repeated a number of times.

Long-Term Memory

If short-term memories are what your brain holds for small amounts of time, long-term memories are the ones you carry around with you for days, months, and years. Long-term memories are created by neurons sending signals across gaps called synapses. The more these signals are repeated, the more the pathways that carry the signals are strengthened—a process that creates long-term memories. There are two categories of long-term memories.

Procedural Memories

These are your "how" memories, which include any skill you've ever learned, from simple tasks such as chewing and walking, to more complex skills such as tying up your shoelaces. Procedural memories rely on your senses, such as knowing how much pressure to put on your shoelaces to tie them up tightly, or how to hold a cup to your mouth to take in water and swallow it without spilling it like a baby does.

PUT YOUR BRAIN TO IT!

Think about your day, from the time you wake up to the time you go to sleep. How many procedural memories do you rely on to get through the day? Make a list and share it with a partner or peer.

Declarative Memories

Declarative or explicit memories are your "what" memories. These are your memories of things—whether they are events such as your first day of school, or of a movie that you saw a few months ago.

In the creation of declarative or explicit memories, your senses are also in play, because in creating these memories, your brain uses all of your senses. For example, a memory of a carnival might include the smell of popcorn, the sound of the crowd, the sight of bright lights, and even the texture and taste of cotton candy.

Your declarative memories can be broken down into two more categories. Semantic memories are all the facts that you've stored, such as knowing the capital city of Italy. Your episodic memory is composed of all the things you've done over time, such as going to a friend's birthday party when you were six.

BRAIN LAB

7 NUMBERS

Most phone numbers are "chunked" into seven digits (with an area code), because this makes them easier to remember.

Have a friend write down a string of seven numbers on a piece of paper. Take a quick look, then put the paper away and take a few breaths. Try writing down the numbers you saw on the paper. Did you get them right?

To get the number into your long-term memory, you may need to look at it longer, and say the numbers aloud several times, until you think you've got them right. Then, take a break, maybe even for half the day. Try to recall the numbers. Can you transfer the numbers, in proper order, from short-term to long-term memory?

5842289

WRAP IT UP!

Your brain is at the center of everything you do. You've learned that your abilities to hear, see, smell, taste, and touch all rely on your brain's ability to process signals coming from your sensory receptors. Both your CNS and PNS work to carry those signals to and from your brain and other parts of your body. You've also learned that your brain is responsible for your speech, memory, emotions, and reactions to the world around you. Check out this diagram to help you remember these functions and which parts of the brain control them.

Sensory cortexes – These process information from skin receptors and body movements

FRONTAL LOBE

Gustatory cortex – This cortex, which controls your sense of taste, is made up of two substructures, one of which is located in the temporal lobe and the other in the frontal lobe

Broca's area – This part of your brain, located in the frontal lobe, processes speech and writing

Olfactory cortex – Responsible for your sense of smell, this cortex is found in the temporal lobes

PARIETAL LOBE

Auditory cortex – Part of the temporal lobe, this controls how you recognize and understand sounds

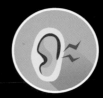

Wernickle's area – Found in the temporal lobe, this is the part of your brain that decodes speech

TEMPORAL LOBE

OCCIPITAL LOBE

Visual cortex – Located in the occipital lobe of the cerebrum, this cortex helps you make sense of what you see

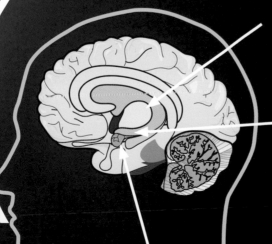

Thalamus – This relays sensory information from your receptors to the cerebrum

Hippocampus – Located in the temporal lobe, the hippocampus is part of the limbic system, and stores your long- and short-term memories

CEREBELLUM

Amygdala – Located in the limbic system deep within the brain, the amygdala controls your emotional reactions to stimuli and events

BIBLIOGRAPHY

BOOKS

Chudler, Eric, and Lise Johnson. *Brain Bytes*. W.W. Norton & Company, 2017.

Cracknell, James. *Body Science*. Dorling Kindersley Limited, 2009.

DK Publishing, *Open Me Up*. DK Books, 2009.

Evans-Marin, Fay. *The Nervous System*. Chelsea House Publishers, 2005.

Gibb, Barry J. *The Rough Guide to the Brain, 2nd Edition*. Rough Guides, 2012.

Ingram, Jay, and Silvia Funston. *It's All in Your Head: A Guide to Your Brilliant Brain*. Maple Tree Press, 1994.

Simons, Ronald C. *Boo! Culture, Experience, and the Startle Reflex*. Oxford University Press, 1996.

Swanson, Diane. *Hmm? The most interesting book you'll ever read about memory*. Kids Can Press, 2001.

Sweeney, Michael S. *Brain: The Complete Mind*. National Geographic, 2009.

WEBSITES

https://faculty.washington.edu/chudler/facts.html

www.theatlantic.com/health/archive/2014/01/the-shape-of-your-head-and-the-shape-of-your-mind/282578/

www.npr.org/sections/13.7/2013/12/02/248089436/the-truth-about-the-left-brain-right-brain-relationship

www.ncbi.nlm.nih.gov/pubmedhealth/PMHT0025455/

www.vivo.colostate.edu/hbooks/pathphys/digestion/basics/gi_nervous.html

www.wired.com/2011/03/language-and-blind-brains/

www.scientificamerican.com/article/what-is-synesthesia/

http://pages.jh.edu/~jhumag/996web/touch.html

http://nba.uth.tmc.edu/neuroscience/s2/chapter06.html

www.ncbi.nlm.nih.gov/pmc/articles/PMC3322418/

https://news.nationalgeographic.com/news/2014/03/140321-nose-human-smell-odors-trillion-science/

www.ncbi.nlm.nih.gov/pubmedhealth/PMH0072592/

https://science.howstuffworks.com/life/inside-the-mind/emotions/fear.htm

www.ncbi.nlm.nih.gov/pmc/articles/PMC3350748/

LEARNING MORE

BOOKS

Chudler, Eric H. *Inside Your Brain*. Chelsea House Publishers, 2007.

Mason, Paul. *Your Mind-Bending Brain and Networking Nervous System*. Crabtree Publishing Company, 2016.

Simpson, Kathleen. *The Human Brain: Inside Your Body's Control Room*. National Geographic, 2009.

WEBSITES

Read about the central and peripheral nervous systems at KidsHealth.org

kidshealth.org/en/parents/brain-nervous-system.html

Get some helpful brain facts—and hear how to pronounce all that difficult brain-related vocabulary—at this site:

faculty.washington.edu/chudler/nsdivide.html

Use this interactive diagram to check out different views of the brain and its parts.

www.koshland-science-museum.org/explore-the-science/ interactives/brain-anatomy

GLOSSARY

auditory nerve The nerve that carries hearing signals from the cochlea of the inner ear to the brain

axon The long, threadlike part of a neuron that sends messages to other neurons

brainstem The central and rearmost part of the brain that connects to the spinal cord

cell body The part of a cell that carries its nucleus, which contains it's genetic information

cell membranes Membranes, or covers, that protect cells from their surroundings

cochlea The part of the inner ear that transmits sound vibrations to the auditory nerve

cornea The clear front part of the eye that covers the pupil, iris, and anterior chamber

dendrites The short, branch-like fibers that extend from the body of a nerve cell, and which receive and transmit messages to the nerve cell from other nerve cells

enzyme A substance that speeds up a chemical reaction, and which is essential for chemical reactions that occur in nerve cells and other cells of the body

facial nerve The nerve that controls facial and tongue movements

glial cells Cells that surround neurons and support them by keeping them in place, insulating them, and providing them with nutrients

glossopharyneal nerve The cranial nerve that carries information from the tongue and throat to the brainstem, and from the brainstem to tongue and throat muscles

gray matter Darker tissue of the brain that contains cell bodies of neurons and their dendrites

gustatory cortex The part of the brain that works with the taste buds to interpret tastes

gyri The ridges on the outer layer of the brain

hormones Substances produced in the body's endocrine glands, and which regulate functions of the body, such as growth and the use of sugar and other carbohydrates

inorganic salts Any salts that do not come from plant or animal matter

matter Anything that takes up space and has mass

mechanoreceptors A type of receptor that responds to stimuli such as touch and sound

medulla The part of the brain responsible for involuntary actions such as sneezing

mucus A sticky substance secreted by mucous membranes and glands to lubricate and protect parts of the body

myelin The fatty substance that encases axons or nerve fibers

neurotransmitter Chemical messengers that transmit messages across the synapses between the axons of nerve cells and dendrites of neighboring nerve cells, or between the axons of nerve cells and adjacent muscle cells

nociceptor A receptor on a nerve cells that transmits messages about potentially harmful stimuli, such as excessive heat, pressure, or an injurious chemical substance

nutrients Substances that provide nourishment, or help a living thing grow

olfactory bulb A structure in the brain that receives signals about smells detected by the cells in the nose

olfactory neurons Cells within the olfactory system, which transmit messages to and from the nose and the brain

optic nerve A nerve in the eye that transmits signals from the retina to the brain

photoreceptors Cells in the eye that convert light into signals to send to the brain

pons The part of the brainstem that links the thalamus and the medulla

proteins Nutrients that consist of amino acids, and which are present in the muscle and other tissues of animals, and in soybeans, peas, kale, and many other plants

retina Tissue at the back of the eye that receives light that the lens has focused, converts it into signals, and sends them to the brain for visual recognition

sensory receptors Special neurons that respond to changes in the environment

soluble organic Substances Organic, or natural, substances that can be dissolved

somatosensory cortex The part of the brain that receives sensory information

stimuli Things that causes a response in a nerve or other cell, tissue, or organ

synapse The gap between nerve cells; messages are sent along the synapse from one cell to another

synesthesia A neurological condition in which each sense is combined with another sense

taste receptor cells The nerve cells in the tongue that send messages to the glossopharyngeal nerve and then to the gustatory cortex of the brain

thermoreceptors Sense receptors that detect changes in temperature

ulnar nerve The nerve that runs near the surface of the skin at the elbow

vagus nerve The cranial nerve that extends from the brain to the abdomen, and carries messages to and from the brain to the digestive tract, heart, lungs, and other organs

white matter The lighter brain tissue that connects the gray matter areas and carries signals between neurons

About the Authors

Jeff Szpirglas and Danielle Saint-Onge work both as authors and teachers. Jeff has written numerous books for young readers focusing on themes such as fear, and unusual human behavior. He is also passionate about horror stories. When taking a break from being a school librarian and writing books, Danielle runs her own private coaching practice, working one-on-one with children and families experiencing executive functioning difficulties. Both Jeff and Danielle are passionate educators who believe in writing books that reflect the experiences and lives of the students they teach.